Dream big.

This book is dedicated to my mother, who taught me its

lesson, and to Cole, Kent and Grant, who live it every day.

I Know
You Can Do It,
You Know
You Can, Too!

Elena Schietinger

When you look in the mirror
each day after night,
just tell yourself
that your future's so bright.

A big world awaits you,

its arms opened wide,

so much you can do

if only you try.

Your dreams are an image

of what your heart wants to be,

the stars shine upon you,

such glory you'll see!

For the first part of magic

is a dream that you make,

in your mind and your soul,

of the paths you will take.

Will you climb a huge mountain?

Or soar through the sky?

Will you make the world better?

You will, if you try!

For the world is just waiting

to see what you'll do,

the energy you'll harness,

the dreams you'll make true.

Your mind is this beautiful

constellation of thoughts,

and your spirit will soar

from all you've been taught.

And if you should find

that you trip on your way,

just brush yourself off

and begin a new day.

For the sun's in the sky

just shining for you,

and all those who love you

know what you can do!

The world waits and watches

to see you shine bright.

You are hope, you are wonder,

you cast a bright light.

You have power and wisdom,

nothing to fear,

the Universe is calling,

its message is clear.

So take a few steps

on this brand new bright day,

chart out your course,

let stars guide your way.

Take all those dear dreams

and make them come true.

I know you can do it,

you know you can too!

So go on and do

all that's waiting for you!

The End.

Archway Publishing books may be ordered through booksellers or by contacting:

Archway Publishing
1663 Liberty Drive
Bloomington, IN 47403
www.archwaypublishing.com
1 (888) 242-5904

Because of the dynamic nature of the Internet, any web addresses or links contained in this book may have changed since publication and may no longer be valid. The views expressed in this work are solely those of the author and do not necessarily reflect the views of the publisher, and the publisher hereby disclaims any responsibility for them.

Any people depicted in stock imagery provided by Getty Images are models, and such images are being used for illustrative purposes only.
Certain stock imagery © Getty Images.

ISBN: 978-1-4808-8384-0 (sc)
ISBN: 978-1-4808-8383-3 (hc)
ISBN: 978-1-4808-8385-7 (e)

Print information available on the last page.

Archway Publishing rev. date: 1/30/2020

Printed in the United States
By Bookmasters